WILD! Exploring Animal Habitats

CREATURES IN A HOT DESERT

Francine Topacio

PowerKiDS press
New York

Published in 2020 by The Rosen Publishing Group, Inc.
29 East 21st Street, New York, NY 10010

Editor: Elizabeth Krajnik
Book Design: Reann Nye

Photo Credits: Cover Vaclav Sebek/Shutterstock.com; Series Art Lilu330/Shutterstock.com; p. 5 Anton Foltin/Shutterstock.com; p. 6 wanida tubtawee/Shutterstock.com; p. 7 rattiya lamrod/Shutterstock.com; p. 8 Ralf Liebhold/Shutterstock.com; p. 9 maloff/Shutterstock.com; p. 10 dorimoreno1/RooM/Getty Images; p. 11 Mrinal Pal/Shutterstock.com; p. 12 Casey K. Bishop/Shutterstock.com; p. 13 Kristian Bell/ Moment Open/Getty Images; p. 14 visuelldesign/Shutterstock.com; p. 15 ColbyJoe/iStock / Getty Images Plus/Getty Images; p. 17 Jay Pierstorff/iStock / Getty Images Plus/Getty Images; p. 18 Judith Lienert/Shutterstock.com; p. 19 Birds and Dragons/Shutterstock.com; p. 20 Elizabeth W. Kearley/Moment/Getty Images; p. 21 Erni/Shutterstock.com; p. 22 JeniFoto/Shutterstock.com.

Library of Congress Cataloging-in-Publication Data

Names: Topacio, Francine, author.
Title: Creatures in a hot desert / Francine Topacio.
Description: New York : PowerKids Press, [2020] | Series: Wild! Exploring animal habitats | Includes index.
Identifiers: LCCN 2019003543| ISBN 9781725304321 (paperback) | ISBN 9781725304345 (library bound) | ISBN 9781725304338 (6 pack)
Subjects: LCSH: Desert animals--Juvenile literature. | Habitat (Ecology)--Juvenile literature.
Classification: LCC QL116 .T67 2020 | DDC 591.754--dc23
LC record available at https://lccn.loc.gov/2019003543

Manufactured in the United States of America

CPSIA Compliance Information: Batch #CSPK19. For Further Information contact Rosen Publishing, New York, New York at 1-800-237-9932.

CONTENTS

DESERT BASICS

A desert is an arid, or very dry, place with little vegetation, or plant life. To be considered a desert, a place must receive less than 10 inches (25 cm) of rain each year. The driest desert on Earth, the Atacama in Chile, gets less than 0.004 inches (0.01 cm) of rain each year on average.

Deserts are found on every **continent**. Some deserts, such as the Sahara in Africa, are dry and hot while others, such as the Gobi Desert in Asia, are always cold. Not all deserts look the same. Some are sandy and others are rocky or mountainous.

Creature Corner

Many people think deserts are places with little life. However, deserts have many species, or kinds, of highly **adapted** plants and animals.

The United States has four large deserts, which are the Mojave, the Sonoran, the Great Basin, and the Chihuahuan. These saguaro cacti are in the Sonoran Desert.

HARSH PLACES

Deserts make up more than one-fifth of Earth's land. So what grows in these **harsh** places? Desert plants don't need much water and have adaptations, such as long roots or **shallow** and broad roots that take in water from the ground. Others store water in their fleshy leaves.

Many desert plants, such as this plant called a succulent, have a waxy coating on their fleshy leaves to keep them cool and to keep them from losing too much water.

Some desert plants only open their stomata, or holes on their leaves, at night so they lose less water. They take in a gas called carbon dioxide and store it until there's sunlight to carry out **photosynthesis**. Many desert plants have spines, or thorns, or make toxins to protect, or guard, themselves from predators. Grasses, bushes, and small trees also grow in deserts.

MAMMALS IN THE DESERT

Desert animals have adaptations to survive in these harsh **environments**, too. There are lots of **mammals** in the desert. One of the main ways mammals, and other animals, survive in hot deserts is staying out of the sun. They are most active at night when it's not as hot.

Creature Corner

Camels, which live in the deserts of Africa and Asia, can drink up to 30 gallons (114 L) of water at one time. They are able to go about a week without drinking.

Peccaries live in deserts in southern parts of North America, Central America, and South America. They eat agaves and prickly pears, which store a lot of water.

Many small mammals, such as the kangaroo rat, dig **burrows** to keep cool and get all or most of the water they need from the foods they eat. Some large mammals with fur, such as coyotes, lose their winter coats in the spring to keep their bodies cool in the summer.

MEERKATS

Meerkats are squirrel-sized burrowing mammals that live in parts of the Kalahari Desert in southern Africa. They live together in groups of up to 40 members.

Meerkats take turns acting as the guard. When the others hear the warning call, they take cover.

Meerkats spend five to eight hours searching for food each day, but spend the afternoon in their burrows to stay cool. Their diet, or food they eat, is made up of bugs, spiders, small **rodents**, lizards, eggs, and **scorpions**.

While eating, meerkats look around to see if predators, such as jackals or raptors, are nearby. One meerkat acts as a guard, standing on its back legs and whistling to tell the others when a predator is near.

REPTILES IN THE DESERT

Many **reptiles** live in deserts around the world. Reptiles are cold blooded, which means their body **temperature** changes with the temperature of their environment. Reptiles that are nocturnal, or mostly active at night, such as most snakes, take in heat from the air and ground. Reptiles that are diurnal, or mostly active during the day, such as some lizards, spend most of the day **basking** in the heat of the sun.

Some reptiles, such as the desert iguana, can have fairly high body temperatures, which can be as high as 108°F (42°C).

Creature Corner

The sandfish, or desert skink, is a reptile that lives in the sandy deserts of North Africa and the Middle East. It spends most of its life in the sand and only comes to the surface to eat, poop, and make babies.

However, reptiles also need to stay cool when the sun gets too hot. Some reptiles, such as turtles and tortoises dig burrows, others move to a different basking area, and others change their skin color.

RATTLESNAKES

Rattlesnakes are venomous, or poisonous, snakes that live in many places in North and South America. The rattle sound they make comes from rings at the end of their tail hitting each other. The rattlesnake makes this sound to warn predators.

Creature Corner

Rattlesnakes are a type of pit viper because they have a small pit between their eyes and nostrils that allows them to sense the heat from their **prey's** body.

The Mojave rattlesnake is highly venomous. It is sometimes known as the Mojave green and has a dark diamond pattern along its back and white and black bands on its tail.

During the day, rattlesnakes hide from the sun in burrows or under rocks. Most are nocturnal and hunt their prey, which includes small mammals such as rodents and lizards, in the early evening. Adult rattlesnakes need to eat only about once every two weeks. Rattlesnakes kill their prey by striking it and pushing their sharp, venom-filled fangs into their prey's body.

THE GILA MONSTER

The Gila monster is a species of venomous lizard that lives in the Mojave, Sonoran, and Chihuahuan deserts of the southwestern United States and northwestern Mexico. They have black bodies with pink, orange, or yellow markings. Gila monsters grow to be about 20 inches (50 cm) long.

Gila monsters spend about 95 percent of their lives in their burrows. They only come out to eat and bask. They are slow predators and hunt at night, eating small mammals, birds, and eggs. Gila monsters store fat in their tails and bellies for the winter and can go months without eating.

Gila monsters have a very strong bite. To put venom into its prey, a Gila monster holds onto its prey with its teeth and chews. Once its prey is dead, the Gila monster swallows it whole.

BIRDS IN THE DESERT

Deserts are home to many species of birds. Some birds, such as the Gila woodpecker, spend their whole lives in the desert. They make their nests by making a hole in a saguaro cactus. However, some move north in winter. Other birds, such as the elf owl, live in holes the woodpeckers have left behind.

GILA WOODPECKER

Turkey vultures eat dead animals. They make their nests in dark places under large rocks, on the edges of cliffs, and in dead trees.

Other birds, such as the phainopepla, **migrate** to deserts for only part of the year. The phainopepla lives and mates, or comes together to make babies, in the Sonoran Desert from February until April and then migrates to forested canyons in Arizona and California to mate again and find more food.

Eagles, hawks, and other large birds fly high above looking for prey. Turkey vultures look for dead animals to eat. They use their strong sense of smell to find rotting meat.

THE GREATER ROADRUNNER

The greater roadrunner is a species of bird that lives in the American Southwest. Roadrunners don't fly very often. Instead, they run at speeds of up to 17 miles (27 km) per hour.

Roadrunners feed on snakes, lizards, spiders, scorpions, bugs, birds, rodents, and bats. They kill their prey by hitting it against the ground or a rock until it dies. If a roadrunner can't find food, it may eat its own young.

Creature Corner

The greater roadrunner can run, fly, and even jump to catch its prey, such as bugs, bats, and hummingbirds, midair.

Roadrunners have black skin under their feathers to take in heat from the sun. They sunbathe in the morning to warm up after a cold night. During the winter months, roadrunners may sunbathe several times a day.

Greater roadrunners mate for life. They build their nests in bushes, low trees, or cacti. Male, or boy, roadrunners gather sticks for the nest, but only the female, or girl, roadrunner builds it.

PROTECTING DESERTS

Even though it might seem like deserts are lifeless, they're actually full of highly adapted life forms. As the sun sets, the desert comes alive. Animals come out to look for food and find mates. The desert is full of life, you just need to know when and where to look!

If you choose to visit a desert you should do your best to keep it the way it is. Don't harm any plants or animals you see. Don't feed the animals and don't leave your trash lying around. Protecting Earth's deserts is important!

GLOSSARY

adapt: To change in order to live better in a certain environment.

bask: To lie in warm surroundings.

burrow: A hole an animal digs in the ground to live or hide.

continent: One of the seven great masses of land on Earth.

environment: The conditions that surround a living thing and affect the way it lives.

harsh: Unpleasant and hard to live in.

mammal: Any warm-blooded animal whose babies drink milk and whose body is covered with hair or fur.

migrate: To move from one area to another for feeding or having babies.

photosynthesis: The process by which green plants turn water and carbon dioxide into food when the plant is in sunlight.

prey: An animal hunted by other animals for food.

reptile: A cold-blooded animal with thin, dry pieces of skin called scales.

rodent: A small, furry animal with large front teeth, such as a mouse or rat.

scorpion: A small animal related to spiders that has two front claws and a curved tail with a poisonous stinger at the end.

shallow: Not deep.

temperature: How hot or cold something is.

INDEX

WEBSITES

Due to the changing nature of Internet links, PowerKids Press has developed an online list of websites related to the subject of this book. This site is updated regularly. Please use this link to access the list: www.powerkidslinks.com/wild/desert